MENTAL TOUGHNESS

Develop an Unbeatable Mind

A. C. Drexel

Table of Contents

INTRODUCTION

I would like to thank you for purchasing this book "Mental Toughness: Develop an Unbeatable Mind."

Mental toughness is the ability to transform promise into actual performance. It is about taking control of your life for making the most of it. It is about understanding that you are the only one that's responsible for your success and no one else can stop you from succeeding. Mental toughness is essential in every aspect of your personal and professional life.

Are there times when a specific situation triggered a negative emotion that hindered your progress? Well, this could be something as simple as a spat with your spouse before heading out to work. When something like this happens, do you feel overwhelmed by the negative emotion and does it take a toll on your productivity and efficiency? If that's the case, then you should learn to let go of all that, and this book will help you with this process!

The information provided in this book is broadly divided into two parts. The first part consists of information about mental toughness and the second part consists of the different things that you can do for becoming mentally tough. In the first section, you will find information about what mental toughness is. It is all about the characteristics of mentally tough people, certain habits that you should develop, the difference between being mentally tough and acting tough, myths about mentally tough people and the things that you shouldn't do if you want to become mentally strong. In the second part, you will learn what emotional intelligence is, the three methods for growing mentally and emotionally tough and all the different traits that you should work on acquiring and developing. Follow the simple tips that have been given in this book, and you can see a positive change in yourself! So, are you ready to get started now?

Section One:

Traits of the Unbeatable Mind

CHAPTER 1:
MENTAL TOUGHNESS

You might be wondering if mental toughness is a trait that can be passed on. Is it something that can be inherited? Something that you are born with? Or can you develop mental toughness? Well, the good news is that it is a trait that can be developed by anyone. The only condition is that you will need to be willing to put in all the effort it takes to achieve a mind that's tough. Right now, you must be thinking that it isn't possible. You might be surrounded by people who seem to be getting everything they ever wished for. Maybe a friend got into the college they chose, they got chosen for the college team, got their dream job, or something else. Does it seem like everyone is getting what they ever wanted, except for you? There you are, hoping for the same things, but you aren't able to enjoy the same opportunities.

There is a reason why things aren't working your way, and it is related to your mental toughness. If someone were to ask you how you would describe your attitude and your passion towards the goals you have set for yourself, what would you say? Is your goal the only thing on your mind or is it something that you wish for? We all have plenty of wishes, and they won't come true until you devise a plan of action to make them come true. If you know that you are genuinely passionate about something, then your mindset towards it changes as well. You will automatically find the drive and the necessary motivation to make your goal become a reality. You will see yourself putting in extra effort to achieve your goals. Have you ever come across a person who doesn't seem to have a lot of talent for something, but who seems to be good at it? Well, skill isn't everything. Passion and perseverance are equally necessary if you want to achieve the goal that you have set for yourself. Mental toughness is the deciding factor that distinguishes between those who are good and those who are great. It is an essential factor, and it can even outweigh any inherent talent.

Developing mental toughness is very important given that we are living in an extremely competitive world. There are certain traits that all those who are mentally tough seem to possess. They are highly motivated; they have a positive mindset, they have self-control, are aware of themselves, can deal well with pressure and are energetic. These people are dynamic and won't let anything or anyone hold them back. If you want to be successful in life, then you will need to develop a mental attitude that keeps you going. You need to make sure that you are trying your best and if things don't go your way, don't get disappointed. Instead, think of it as a learning opportunity and do everything that you can to make sure that you achieve your goals. Learn to adapt yourself to the situation and don't let your emotions get the better of you. If you have a goal or a dream that you want to achieve, then you will have to start making a plan and take the necessary action to achieve it. Come up with a plan of action and don't let anything in between you and your goal. Be flexible and don't be rigid. Put in all the effort that you can and then some more. Keep going and don't give up. You will learn more about developing mental toughness in the coming chapters.

CHAPTER 2:
CHARACTERISTICS OF MENTALLY TOUGH PEOPLE

We all would have come across specific points in our lives where our mental toughness was put to the test. It might have come in the form of a toxic friendship, a dead-end job or a destructive relationship. Regardless of what the challenge is, you need to be strong, change your perspective towards life, and be proactive if you want to be successful. It sounds pretty simple, doesn't it? Who wouldn't want good friends, a happy relationship and a satisfactory job? It might seem easy, but it takes a lot of hard work. It isn't easy to be mentally tough when you feel like you are stuck. The ability to break free of the bonds holding you back and creating your path takes courage that only those who are mentally tough possess. It is fascinating to see the way in which mentally tough people set themselves aside from everyone else. Where others see an impossible hurdle to cross, they see a challenge that needs to be overcome.

In the year 1914, Thomas Edison's factory burned down, and several precious prototypes were destroyed, and the damage amounted to $23 million. Edison's reply to this unfortunate incident was "Thank goodness all our mistakes were burned up. Now we can start fresh again." Edison's response sums up what mental toughness is about. It is about having a positive outlook towards life, seeing opportunities, and taking the necessary action even when things start looking bleak. There are a couple of characteristics that all those who are mentally tough share and they are as follows.

They are emotionally intelligent

One of the building blocks of mental toughness is emotional intelligence. If you cannot understand and tolerate negative emotions and turn them into something productive, then you cannot be mentally tough. Moments that put your mental toughness to test are testing your emotional quotient as well. Your IQ or intelligence quotient is fixed, whereas your EQ, or your emotional quotient (emotional intelligence), isn't and it can be improved if you are willing to work on it. Emotional intelligence is a highly desirable trait, and all those who are successful have a high EQ. When you can analyze a situation objectively and not emotionally, you will be able to make a better decision. If you can be easily swayed by positive and negative emotions, you are opening yourself up for manipulation.

They are very confident

Henry Ford once said, "Whether you think you can, or think you can not- you're right." Your mentality can influence your ability to achieve success. Mentally tough people will firmly believe in Ford's notion. If you don't feel confident about yourself and your skills, you cannot expect someone else to feel confident about you. Real confidence is essential and not false bravado. People often tend to mask their insecurities by merely projecting confidence, instead of being confident. A confident person will always stand apart when compared to all those who are indecisive, doubtful, and skittish. Their confidence often inspires others as well.

They are good at neutralizing toxic people

It is not only exhausting but also quite frustrating to deal with difficult people. People who are mentally tough are capable of taking control of their interactions with toxic elements around them. A mentally tough person can keep his or her emotions in check while confronting a toxic person. Their approach would often be rational. If you want to be mentally strong, then you should be able to identify negative emotions like anger and shouldn't let these feelings get the better of you. Negativity simply adds fuel to the fire, and it doesn't take long for the situation to spin out of your control rapidly. Take a moment and try to see the problematic person's point of view as well and try finding some common ground or a solution to the problem.

Even when things are going south, a mentally tough person will be able to prevent the toxic person from bringing them down.

They can embrace change

Mentally tough people are quite dynamic and are capable of embracing change. They not only embrace change but can adapt themselves to any situation as well. They are well aware of the fact that the fear of change can stall their progress and prevent them from achieving success. A mentally tough person would look for any likely change and devise a plan of action that will help him or her in making the most of the possible change. If you don't embrace change, then you will never see any good in it. Keep an open mind and check for ways in which you can capitalize on such change. You will be setting yourself up for failure if you keep doing things in the same way while ignoring any changes. Ignoring it or avoiding it will not make it go away. So, stop doing the same thing over and over again and expect a different outcome. Well, that indeed is the definition of insanity.

They can say no

If you want to reduce your chances of experiencing stress and depression, then learn to say "no." Saying "no" is, in fact, good for your mental health. All those who are mentally tough possess the self-esteem and the foresight that helps them say no. If you have trouble saying "no" to others, then you should start working on it immediately. Saying "no" not only helps you in avowing unnecessary burden, but it will also help you in prioritizing your work and cutting off toxic people from your life. While saying no, a mentally strong person would steer clear of phrases like "I don't think" or "I am not certain." Whenever you are saying no, say it with confidence. Learning to say no will help a person to concentrate better on the tasks they have on hand instead of taking on more work that they might be able to honor. The ones who are mentally tough have good self-control, and they can say "no" not just to others, but to themselves as well. Stop taking action impulsively and instead follow the rules of delayed gratification.

"No" is quite a powerful word and it can help you in protecting your valuable time. When you have to say "no," just say it. Don't make use of phrases like "I am not sure," "I don't think I will be able to" and so on. If you won't be able to take on any additional commitments or if you feel that you have got a lot of work to do, then don't take on any new obligations. Just say no. If you get stuck with something that you won't be able to do, then this will only create additional stress, pressure, and just burn you out eventually. Learn how to say no, and this will help in improving your productivity.

They know that fear causes regret

If you never take a chance, you will never know what could have happened. Unless you try, you wouldn't know.

Instead of lamenting over the opportunities you didn't take, it is better to control your fears and make the leap. Don't be afraid of taking risks. However, this doesn't mean that you will take on any risk blindly. What is the worst thing that can ever happen to you? Death isn't the answer. The worst thing is regret. Regret about the things that you could have and should have done. Regret can eat you up from within. Mentally tough people know that fear causes disappointment, and this is where self-awareness steps in. Self-Awareness will help you in balancing between dwelling and remembering. Dwelling for too long on your mistakes will make you anxious and conscious, whereas forgetting about them increases your chances of repeating them all over again. You need to learn to transform your failures and look for an opportunity to improve.

They can embrace failure

Failures are very common, and everyone has their fair share of failures in their lives. Mentally tough people are capable of embracing their failures. No one can experience success without knowing what failure is. When you can acknowledge that you are on the wrong path, are aware of the mistakes you are making, and can embrace your failures, only then will you be able to achieve success.

Letting go of all the wrongs

Mentally tough people are aware that what you concentrate on will determine your emotional state. When you stay fixated on a problem that you are facing, you tend to create and drag on the negative emotions, which in turn stalls your progress. When you start focusing on yourself and the circumstances you are in, you will feel a sense of personal efficacy, which helps in generating positive emotions and improve your productivity. Mentally tough people are capable of distancing themselves from their mistakes without forgetting them. Keep your mistakes at a safe distance, learn and adapt from them, but stop dwelling on them for prolonged periods of time.

No one can limit their joy

If you derive your sense of pleasure and satisfaction from comparing yourself to others, your happiness no longer lies in your own hands. You are essentially giving up the control of your happiness to someone else. Those who are mentally tough would feel good about something regardless of what others think or say. No one can take away your joy or happiness from you. It isn't possible to completely ignore what others think of you. However, you don't have to compare yourself with others. It is better if you take people's opinions with a pinch of salt. People who are mentally strong know that irrespective of what others think of them at any given point of time, one thing is for sure- they are never really as good or bad as others seem to believe. You should stop comparing yourself to others; physically, socially, or even financially. It is a trap that you should be aware of. You will always have people around you who have got more money than you have, have a better social life or are more successful in their respective careers. Instead of focusing on what others have, you should focus on yourself.

They won't limit the happiness of others

A mentally tough person won't be critical of others because he or she knows that everyone has something different to offer. They don't have to bring others down for them to feel good about themselves. By comparing yourself to others, you are only limiting yourself. Jealousy, envy and resentment can drain you out of your energy and suck the life out of you. Mentally tough people will never waste their energy worrying about what others think of them, and they certainly won't spend their energy sizing others up. Instead of allowing all sorts of negative emotions to manifest, you should concentrate on channelizing your energy towards something that's more positive and something beneficial. Celebrate others' successes and rejoice in their victories, it won't diminish your accomplishments. Learn to radiate positivity.

They exercise

Exercising can help you in finding mental, physical, and emotional stability. When you start exercising, you are not only improving your physical health, you are getting rid of negative emotions as well. Start exercising at least thrice a week and you will feel better about yourself. Your self-esteem will get a healthy boost when you can develop your physical image. A person who is mentally tough knows the importance of exercising and will make sure that they are getting their quota of exercise daily. The endorphin high that you experience after exercising can lend your perspective some much-needed positivity.

They get sufficient sleep

Sleep is quite essential if you are trying to improve your mental toughness. While you are sleeping, your brain starts working on removing all the toxic proteins that are produced because of the neural activity that takes place while you are awake. Well, your brain can do this only when you are asleep. So, when you don't get sufficient sleep, there is a build-up of these toxins in your brain, and it affects your ability to think as well. You cannot fix this by increasing your caffeine intake. A mentally tough person knows that their overall productivity and focus are all adversely affected when they don't get sufficient sleep or when they don't get the right kind of rest. So, sleep needs to be a priority if you want to make yourself mentally strong. Think about it for a moment. Do you or don't you feel fresher and more energetic after getting a good night's sleep? Don't you feel cranky and agitated if you don't sleep or have had a disturbed sleep? Your outlook can drastically change depending on whether you have slept or not.

Their caffeine intake isn't excessive

Excessive consumption of caffeine increases the production of adrenaline in the body. Adrenaline is the hormone that is responsible for our flight or fight response. This mechanism can override our ability to reason. Once this response is triggered in our body, the primary focus of the body is shifted towards survival and self-preservation, and everything else becomes secondary. It is good when you are in a life-threatening situation, but not so great when you have a hurdle to overcome. The caffeine you keep consuming will automatically shift your body into a state of hyper-awareness of every emotion you feel. Your emotions will start getting a hold on you and rationality will go right out of the window. The initial caffeine rush that you experience would certainly help you in doing your work, however, as it starts wearing off slowly, you will feel agitated and anxious. A mentally strong person knows that they don't need excessive caffeine to help them get through the day. They are aware of the extreme damage caffeine can do to them.

They don't need an apology to forgive others

A mentally tough person knows that life does get easier when you let go of all grudges and start forgiving all those who wronged you. They don't wait for an apology to forgive others. They are capable of forgiving others without an apology, and that's why they seem happier than the rest. You will feel lighter and more relaxed when you let go of some of the hatred you might be harboring towards others or any other ill feelings. All these negative emotions will bring you down and destroy your peace of mind. Negative feelings are similar to parasites that should be squashed. Holding a grudge against someone takes up a lot of your energy and creates more stress. Holding on to a grudge just increases this pressure that can manifest itself in physical and mental forms. When you forgive others, you aren't condoning their actions; instead, it just means that you have reduced your unnecessary emotional baggage.

They are always positive

Reading news these days has become a sad affair. Mass killings, suicide bombings, violence, crippling economies, failing companies, and plenty of environmental mishaps. Phew, that is a lot of negativity to go through. In times like these, it is quite easy to give up on a positive attitude. A mentally tough person wouldn't worry about all that for a simple reason. He or she cannot control any of those things. However, their attitude is something that they can control, and that's what they would concentrate on. They wouldn't waste their energies on something that cannot be helped. Instead, try utilizing your energy to do something good, and it might be helpful.

Mental toughness isn't a quality that only a few are blessed with. You can achieve it with some effort.

CHAPTER 3:
MYTHS ABOUT MENTALLY STRONG PEOPLE

We all talk a lot about physical strength, but in this process, we tend to forget about mental toughness as well. Because of this, there are a couple of misconceptions that exist about being mentally strong. In this chapter, the most famous myths about being mentally strong have been debunked.

Myth #1: They were all born strong

Babies aren't naturally born with Hulk-like super strength, are they? Similarly, no one is born with a lot of mental strength. Mental toughness is something that needs to be acquired and then developed. It is like any other cognitive or behavioral skill that can be learned. Improving your mental strength will take a lot of effort, practice and commitment. It wouldn't be easy to give up on the habits that hold you back, but we all can improve our mental strength.

Myth #2: They are devoid of emotions

A person who is mentally strong isn't cold or devoid of all feelings. They experience emotions just like all of us, but they are aware of the manner in which their feelings can influence their behavior and actions. They can control their feelings and can respond to a situation without reacting immediately. It helps them in reaching their goals and is quite helpful. They aren't aloof or distant; they are practical and rational. They are well aware of the consequences that follow when they let their emotions guide them.

Myth #3: They are very aggressive

Mentally strong people don't expend their energy thinking about how they can please everyone around them. They certainly don't try controlling others and aren't bossy or aggressive. Instead, they are good at taking up the responsibility for how they behave and wouldn't like to waste their time doing something as petty as manipulating others.

Myth #4: They don't know what hardship is

A person doesn't become mentally tough without overcoming their fair share of difficulties in life. Everyone has particular hardships in life, and there is no way in which you can compare any two. The thing that differentiates those who are mentally strong from everyone else is their ability to overcome hardships without getting bogged down by it. They would never use their misfortunes as an excuse for not accomplishing their goals, and they would instead make use of their experience for growing stronger. They believe that every obstacle is a learning experience and they always look for something positive instead of concentrating on all the negatives.

Myth #5: They don't ask for help

A mentally strong person won't shy away from asking for help. If they don't know something, they are capable of accepting the same, and they won't hesitate in doing so. They are willing to seek help when they need it. It is okay to ask for help when they don't know what they are doing and a mentally strong person would do so without letting their ego or pride take hold of them. They would never shame anyone who might seek help either.

Myth #6: They don't have any mental health problems

Mental health and mental strength are different concepts altogether. Forever, it is a popular misconception that they are the same things. People wrongly assume that a person with health problems cannot be mentally strong and vice versa. Some people are mentally tough because they have overcome specific mental health problems. Overcoming mental health problems like anxiety and depression helps in strengthening a person mentally.

Myth #7: They take pride in ignoring pain

Being mentally strong doesn't necessarily mean that they don't feel any pain. How can a human being not feel any pain? That's just not possible. However, a mentally strong individual knows how to motor through slight discomfort if it brings him or her a step closer towards their goal.

Well, mentally tough people, like everyone else, are misunderstood quite often. So, don't worry about losing touch with your emotional side just to become stronger mentally. To grow mentally strong, the emotional and rational parts of the brain need to be in complete harmony.

CHAPTER 4:
DIFFERENCE BETWEEN MENTALLY STRONG AND ACTING TOUGH

There is a significant difference between acting tough and being mentally strong. A controlling supervisor at work, an incredibly demanding boss, bossy co-worker, or even an aggressive customer might be masking their lack of mental toughness by putting up a façade of toughness. Acting might help in improving someone's success initially, but not forever. However, for how long can a person keep faking? Mental strength is essential in the long run, and it cannot be faked. A successful person didn't rise to the top by feigning toughness. Instead, their success is associated with their mental strength. The stronger they are, the higher are their chances to succeed. Grit and persistence are necessary to become a top performer in any avenue. Along with this, there needs to be a desire to keep improving. In this chapter, let us take a look at the differences between being mentally tough and acting tough.

Tough people are of the opinion that failure isn't an option

It is highly unlikely that you will always be successful. Failure is a part of achieving success. Striving for success is a healthy attitude, but if you start believing that you always need to succeed on the first attempt itself, you are setting yourself up for failure. A mentally tough person knows that failures are part and parcel of life. They would think of failure as a temporary setback that they need to overcome and with this positive attitude, they will be able to do so quite quickly. A person who is pretending to be tough will be of the opinion that a failure is never an option. This attitude can become quite problematic when things don't go their way.

Faking toughness to mask insecurities

When a person tries to act tough, he or she is trying on a fake persona that seems to say "Hey! Look at me! I am great!" The façade they put up is quite brittle, and it can crumble at any given point of time. That tough exterior is simply a tool to hide their insecurities. It is okay to have certain vulnerabilities; you are human after all. A mentally strong person is aware of his or her vulnerabilities and tries to work on fixing them instead of pretending that they don't exist. You will be able to progress if you try fixing any weaknesses instead of covering them up and then hoping that they will go away.

The "I can do anything" attitude

Being self-confident is important. However, there is a fine line between being self-confident and being cocky or overconfident. Self-confidence will help you in tackling challenging situations, and overconfidence is your shortcut to disappointments and failures. Overestimating your abilities will leave you inadequately equipped for dealing with realities of lie and underestimating the time required for achieving your goals will lead to severe disappointments. Mental strength is about understanding where you stand and what your abilities are. It isn't about having a false sense of bravado that can crack under the slightest pressures. It is about understanding your skills and working hard for achieving the goals you have set for yourself.

Acting tough usually involves a lot of pride

Those who would want to be perceived as being tough always feel that they have something to prove to others. Their self-worth depends on what others think of them. It doesn't depend on their perception of themselves but on what the world thinks of them. An attitude like this can take a toll on the individual. If your happiness is dependent on someone else's opinion, then you can never be satisfied. Becoming mentally tough is all about learning to be humble and understanding your abilities. A person who is mentally strong won't hesitate in asking for help when the need arises. They won't let pride stop them from asking for help or admitting ignorance of something.

"Tough" people tend to ignore their emotions

Concealing emotions is possible for a while. However, this isn't a viable idea in the long run. Ignoring feelings, in the long run, can cause a lot of damage to your mental health. Suppressed emotions tend to wiggle their way to the surface, eventually if not immediately. Not acknowledging your emotions and hoping that they will pass will not do you any good whatsoever. Being strong is all about understanding your emotions and acting rationally after considering those emotions. A person who is acting tough often believes that emotions are a sign of weakness and tends to ignore them. Only if you acknowledge what you feel, will you be able to get control over it.

They thrive on power

All those who act like they are tough, decide to do so because they like being perceived as powerful and in control. Due to this, they often tend to micromanage and boss others around. They also end up having unreasonable expectations and demands. A person who is mentally strong will like to focus their energy on controlling their thoughts and rationalizing their behavior instead of trying to control all other external factors.

Acting tough = Tolerating pain

Becoming mentally tough isn't about tolerating pain. It is about learning from the pain you experience so that you don't have to go through the same thing again. A mentally strong person would like to focus on their overall growth and development and wouldn't treat their body like a machine.

It is not about having a tough exterior, but it is about having a healthy mind that doesn't waver easily. It is about developing mental strength and like any other exercise, it takes practice to improve mental strength.

CHAPTER 5:
THINGS MENTALLY STRONG PEOPLE DON'T DO

In this chapter, you will learn about the things that a mentally strong person doesn't do. By going through the list of things mentioned in this chapter, you can make sure that you don't indulge in any of the following characteristics.

They don't feel sorry for themselves

There is nothing as terrible as self-pity. A mentally strong person won't waste their time or energy by feeling sorry for themselves or by wallowing in self-pity. Instead, they take responsibility for their actions and try to understand how they can improve the situation instead of thinking about how unfair the circumstances are or how poorly others have treated them.

They never give their power away

They would never allow someone else to push their buttons or control their actions. They won't let someone else boss them around or make them feel terrible. A mentally strong person knows that they are in control of their emotions and they can choose the way in which they want to respond in a given situation.

Change doesn't scare them

A person who is mentally strong won't run away from change. Instead, they will embrace it with open arms and will try to be as flexible as they possibly can be. They understand and accept the fact that change is part and parcel of life and there is no possible way in which change can be avoided.

They don't worry about things they can't control

A mentally tough person knows that it is a lost cause to try and control external factors. Instead, a mentally strong person would like to focus on all the things that are in fact within their control. They know that at times the only thing that they can control is their attitude towards the situation.

They don't try to please others

A mentally tough individual knows that they cannot please everyone. They aren't afraid of speaking out their mind when they realize they are being wronged. They certainly won't accept someone else's opinion just because they are scared of displeasing others. You are responsible for your happiness, and a mentally tough person knows this.

They don't get scared of risks

They don't get scared of risks and instead, they take calculated risks. They know their capacity to shoulder a loss, and they would take a risk only when they know that they wouldn't sustain a considerable loss. They believe in making informed decisions.

They let go of their past

A mentally tough person knows that dwelling on the past is a sheer wastage of time that they have. There is no point in sitting and wishing that things could have been different. They embrace their past, learn from their mistakes, and live in the present while preparing for the future. They don't keep reliving their errors or fantasize about the good old days. Live in the present. Stop kicking yourself for the things that you did or didn't do in your past. The past needs to stay in the past. Focus on the present and think about the future.

They don't repeat the same mistakes

Insanity is defined as doing the same thing over and over again, and expecting different results. A mentally strong person will take responsibility for his or her mistakes and will learn from them. An error is a learning opportunity, and they wouldn't keep repeating the same thing again and again. Instead, they use their experience to make better decisions in the future.

They don't resent someone else's success

A mentally strong person is capable of celebrating other people's achievements without any ill feelings. They don't feel jealous or envious of what others have or have achieved. Instead, they willingly partake in the celebrations. A mentally strong individual knows that they need to put in the effort to achieve the success they desire.

They don't give up

Failures are part and parcel of life. They cannot be avoided, and they certainly shouldn't prevent you from taking action in the future. Every failure teaches you something, so learn from it and don't repeat it in the future.

They aren't scared of being on their own

It is okay to be on your own, and a mentally strong person knows this. They don't mind being on their own. Few people are usually scared of being alone with just their thoughts to keep them company. A mentally strong person won't fall under this category. In fact, they can make use of that time to do something productive on their own. Learn to enjoy your company.

They don't feel that the world owes them

A mentally strong person doesn't think that he or she is entitled to things in life. They believe that they are entitled to the things that their effort and hard work will produce. They aren't born with the mentality that others should take care of them. Instead, they actively look for ways in which they can get things on their own. They don't have a sense of entitlement.

Don't expect immediate results

They know that things take time and results cannot be produced overnight. They know how to be patient, and they can wait for the results they want. A mentally strong person will make constructive use of their skills and time to make the most of the situation they are in; instead of focusing on the outcome that they cannot control.

By refraining from doing any of the things mentioned above, you can develop your own mental strength.

Section Two:
Building Mental Strength

CHAPTER 6:
HABITS TO DEVELOP

Mental strength can be developed over a period if you choose to make your development and growth a priority. In the previous chapter, you learned about the things that a mentally strong person will never indulge in. In this chapter, you will learn about the different daily habits of mentally strong individuals that help in making them stronger. Read on to learn more about the various habits.

Judicious use of their mental energy

It is quite easy to get distracted by different thoughts and things. Did you ever start working and get distracted by something that's entirely different? Not everything is essential, and you indeed don't have to exert the same mental energy and focus. A mentally strong person is capable of prioritizing and knows the importance of making proper use of their mental energy to accomplish their goals.

Reframing all negative thoughts

Who doesn't have negative feelings? A mentally strong person knows that there is no point in encouraging negative thoughts and such a person would try to reframe all their negative thoughts into positive ones. Instead of getting discouraged by the negative thoughts, they would think of a way in which they can make it positive. They consciously try to change the pessimistic dialogue in their head to something positive that will encourage them to work harder. Whenever they feel low, they give themselves a pep talk.

Working towards established goals

A mentally strong person always establishes precise personal and professional goals for themselves. They don't believe in immediate gratification and can work towards long-term goals without giving up. Every hurdle that they have to overcome is viewed as a challenge and not a problem.

Reflecting on their progress

A mentally strong person will spend a couple of minutes daily to review their goals and their progress so far. Only when you consider your performance will you understand how well you are doing and the scope for improvement. They are capable of holding themselves responsible for any mistakes they make and will strive for something better.

They can tolerate discomfort

At times, people tend to go to great lengths to avoid any form of pain or distress. A strong person knows to endure a little discomfort if it means they can achieve greater things. It could be something as simple as pushing yourself to exercise after a long and a tiring day at work.

Being grateful

A mentally strong person believes in practicing gratitude daily. They know how fortunate they are and will always count their blessings instead of thinking about all the things they don't have. You should always be grateful for the things you have. Any self-help book that you pick up will tell you the same thing. Appreciate what you have, that's the only way in which you will learn to be happy with yourself.

Balancing emotions and logic

Balancing logic and emotions is important. A mentally strong person realizes the importance of doing this. Such a person won't react to a situation immediately and would instead spend some time to analyze the situation and then respond accordingly. A mentally strong person will never let their emotions get the better of them and will decide rationally.

Living according to their values

You might feel like measuring your self-worth by comparing yourself with others. However, mentally strong people avoid doing anything of this sort. All such comparisons are nothing but unnecessary distractions. Instead, they focus all their energy on doing their best, regardless of the surrounding circumstances. All that matters to them is whether they managed to do something productive or not.

CHAPTER 7:
IMPROVING YOUR EMOTIONAL INTELLIGENCE

Emotional intelligence is referred to as EI, and it is the controversial counterpart to the conventional IQ or Intelligence Quotient. EI refers to the measure of your ability to perceive your emotions, as well as the emotions of those around you, and of managing them in a manner that's productive and healthy. Emotional intelligence is fundamental to our existence, and it can influence your success in personal and professional lives. Regardless of the stage of life, you are at present; you can make use of the simple steps that have been mentioned in this chapter to develop your emotional intelligence.

Step 1: Notice how you feel

While we are busy rushing from one commitment or obligation to the next one, meeting multiple deadlines and responding to different demands, most of us tend to lose touch with our inner selves and our conscience. We lose touch with our emotions, and when this happens, our minds switch on the autopilot mode automatically. It means that we end up missing out on relevant information that our emotions tend to contain. Whenever you have an emotional reaction to someone, something, or a situation, you are in fact receiving information about that person, thing or event. The reaction that we tend to experience is due to the present situation, or it is perhaps the reaction to a past event or an unprocessed memory. When you start paying attention to what you are feeling, you will be able to start trusting your emotions and this, in turn, will help you in becoming better equipped at managing them. If you are feeling a little lost, then you can try this simple exercise. Set a time for different points during the day. Whenever the timer beeps, take a few deep breaths and concentrate on what you are feeling. Pay attention to the reason that elicited the emotion and notice if there is any physical manifestation of that emotion. The more you practice this, the easier it gets. Noticing what you are feeling will help you in understanding yourself in a better manner.

Step 2: Pay attention to your behavior

Like mentioned above, an important part of developing your emotional intelligence is learning to manage what you feel, which is something you can do only if you are conscious or aware of your emotions. While you are working on your emotional awareness, you should start paying attention to the way you behave as well. Observe how you act while you are experiencing a particular emotion or the manner in which it affects your daily life. Does your behavior have an impact on the way you communicate with others, your efficiency, or your overall wellbeing? Once you are aware of your reaction to certain emotions, it is quite easy to start being judgmental and start attaching different labels to your behavior. Try refraining yourself from indulging in anything of this sort. If you are overly critical of yourself all the time, it is very likely that you will cease being honest about how you feel.

Step 3: Start taking responsibility

One of the most challenging and helpful steps is that you should start taking responsibility for not just how you feel but the way you behave as well. You are the only one that's responsible for your emotions and behaviors. No one else is responsible, and they come from within you. If you feel hurt because of something that someone says or does, and you snap at them, you are responsible for your reaction. They didn't make you snap or lash out; you did it on your own. Since you aren't a puppet, you are the only one responsible for how you feel. What you think about others or a particular situation will provide you with insight about your needs, preferences and expectations. However, remember that no one is responsible for your feelings. Once you accept responsibility for what you feel and how you behave, it will have a positive effect on all the different aspects of your life.

Step 4: Responding instead of reacting

Responding and reacting are often used as synonyms, but there is a subtle difference between these two things. An unconscious process that gets kick started when you experience an emotional trigger is known as the reaction. By reacting, you are relieving or expressing an emotion that was triggered (like feeling irritated with something and lashing out at someone who has interrupted you). Responding, on the other hand, is a conscious process and it involves two steps- observing what you feel, and then deciding the way you want to behave. For instance, you are irritated, and you are explaining to someone how you are feeling and the reason why it isn't a good time to interrupt you.

Step 5: Learn to empathize

When you can understand why someone feels or behaves the way he or she does is known as empathy. When you feel empathetic, you can see the other person's perspective, and you can tell them you understand what they are feeling. Empathy is an important characteristic, and it applies to yourself and others as well. If you want to improve your emotional intelligence, then you need to learn to empathize with yourself and those around you as well. Whenever you feel that you are behaving in a particular manner, ask yourself the reason for your behavior and think about the underlying emotion that triggered such behavior. Your initial response might be "I don't know," but take a moment and think about it, you will know the reason.

Step 6: Creating a positive environment

Once you have started following all the steps mentioned above, you need to take some time for yourself and think about all the positive aspects of your life. Be grateful for everything that's good in your life. Creating a positive environment will help to improve the quality of your life, and it is contagious. If you are radiating positivity, it is bound, rubbing off on those around you as well.

Step 7: It is a continuous process

The process of improving your emotional intelligence is a lifetime practice, and it isn't something that you can develop and then quit. You can keep increasing your EI. Even if you feel like you have got a good hold on all the steps mentioned above, keep practicing. Keep practicing, and you will be able to reap the benefits it offers throughout your life.

CHAPTER 8:
HOW TO BE MENTALLY STRONG

In this section, you will learn about the four methods that you can make use of to become mentally strong. These methods are- identification of challenges and establishing goals, staying even-keeled, developing mental and emotional strength, and dealing with different situations.

Wouldn't it be wonderful if you could deal with all the ups and downs of life with poise and strength? Becoming mentally and emotionally strong is a continuous process, and you cannot achieve it overnight. Every hurdle that you come, across in your life is a learning experience it provides you with an opportunity to practice being mentally strong.

Method One: Identification of Challenges and Establishing Goals

Understanding the meaning of being emotionally resilient

Being mentally strong or tough means that you are capable of adapting yourself to stressful situations or trauma without breaking down. Resilience isn't a characteristic that a person is born with and it is a process that anyone can learn and develop on. Being emotionally tough doesn't mean that you aren't capable of feeling or experiencing any negative emotion or pain. Emotional resilience is always improved in the face of adversity- a painful situation to bounce back from. What does it mean to "bounce back" from such situations or experiences? To develop your emotional resilience, you should be willing to work on improving specific essential skills like the ability of planning and executing the plans, building confidence, self-awareness, managing strong impulses, and the ability to communicate effectively and to solve problems efficiently.

Learning to manage your emotions

If you want to become mentally strong, then you need to learn to manage your emotions. You certainly cannot control what life throws at you, but you can control the way you react to it. You are always in control of your reactions. It isn't an innate quality, and you need to learn to manage your emotions productively. You will learn more about managing and developing certain desirable traits in the coming chapters.

All the challenges you face

Is there anything you would like to change about yourself? Before you can start developing your emotional and mental strength, you should take a while and think about all your strengths, weaknesses, and the challenges that you will need to overcome. Think about all those aspects of your life that you would like to change. Make a list of these things and see how it will help you in achieving your goals. For instance, if one of the challenges is that you want to overcome is the difficulty in asserting your needs and you want to fix this issue, then your immediate goal should be to stop being indecisive and become more assertive. It isn't just about identifying all those areas that you should work on but about celebrating your strengths as well. List down all your positive traits and characteristics. Read through them and celebrate yourself! These favorable attributes will come in handy while achieving your goals.

Take your previous experiences into consideration

One of the reasons why you feel that you lack in mental strength might be linked to something that might have happened in your past. Regardless of how recent or old the incident is, it will affect your mental and emotional strength. For instance, all those children who undergo some form of neglect, abuse, or any other trauma during their childhood tend to develop mental and emotional insecurities while growing up. Take some time and think about any negative experience that you might have experienced in the past that is adding to your emotional or mental state. Consider the reasons as to why and how such incidents might have affected you. If you want, you can always contact a therapist or a counselor about the issues you are facing to get a better understanding of them. Determine if you have an addiction that needs to be remedied. An addiction to drugs, alcohol, tobacco, sex, or anything else that might be threatening your emotional well being. If you think you are addicted to something, try getting rid of it slowly. If interested, you can always seek help for the same. There are plenty of doctors and therapist whom you can consult on this. The first step to tackling a challenge is accepting that you have a problem. If you keep living in denial, there is no way in which you can overcome the challenge that you are facing.

Maintain a journal

It might sound old fashioned, but maintaining a journal will undoubtedly help you. Keeping a journal can assist you in understanding what you might be feeling, the experiences that created such emotions, and it helps in letting go of unnecessary stress as well. It is quite easy to maintain a journal. Just set aside 20 minutes daily to write about your day. You can write about how you are feeling, your thoughts, or anything else. Write about the incidents that bothered you and the emotions you felt. Think about the reasons for such feelings and make a note of it as well. Just write down everything that you think! It doesn't necessarily have to be good or bad. Your journal is the perfect outlet for all the emotions you might be feeling.

Consider talking to a counselor

At times, it might be difficult to figure things out on your own, and you might need a little additional help. If you feel that you are struggling to determine what you are feeling, then consider talking to a therapist or a counselor. There is no shame in accepting that you need some help. It is entirely reasonable to seek help and don't let anyone else tell you otherwise. Your aim should be to become mentally tough and for doing that you will need to overcome all the unresolved issues that you might be dealing with knowingly or unknowingly.

Method Two: Staying Even-keeled

Maintain distance from things that disturb you

If you are trying to cope with any negative emotions by warming up to different vices like drugs, alcohol, or anything destructive, then stop doing that immediately. Stop trying to internalize the negative emotions you feel. If you want to become mentally tough, the first step is to take into consideration all those negative emotions that hinder your performance and productivity. The next time you feel stressed, don't reach for your pack of cigarettes. Instead, think of the reason that is causing you stress and see what you can do about such a thing. Start taking steps to push these vices away from your life. They indeed shouldn't determine how you feel or control the way you act.

Taking good care of yourself

You need to take care of yourself. Maintain a healthy diet, exercise regularly, and give yourself some time for resting and relaxing. It will help in making you feel mentally stronger. By taking good care of your body, you are developing your sense of well being. Your mind will be more relaxed. Start exercising daily for at least 30 minutes; if not daily, then on every alternate day at least. You don't necessarily have to go to the gym to exercise. You can swim, play a sport you like, go for a jog, do some yoga or any other activity that will get your blood pumping. Start eating a healthy and a balanced diet that consists of whole foods, lean proteins, healthy fats, and seasonal fruits and vegetables. A healthy diet will make you feel good about yourself. It is essential that you sleep for at least 7 hours every night. Always keep your body thoroughly hydrated and have at least eight glasses of water per day.

Enrich your mind

Keep challenging and open yourself up to learning all the time. Over a period, you will keep accruing knowledge, and as a result, you will become mentally tougher and wiser. Don't get stuck in a mental or a physical rut. Learn to be curious and well informed about the world. Be a sponge and absorb information. Start reading books, watch good and informative movies, attend concerts and plays, go to the ballet, and start taking an interest in some form of art or the other. Why don't you make some art of your own? You can paint, draw, and learn to play a musical instrument, take up singing, knit, or do anything else that will help you in engaging your inner creativity. It is time to learn some new skills. You can do anything that you want to. Maybe you always wanted a garden of your own, but never got around to it. If that's the case, then there is no time like the present to get started. Talk to lots of people, step out of your comfort zone, go and socialize. Well, there are plenty of things that you can do to enrich your mind.

Concentrate on your spiritual side as well

You can derive strength from paying some attention to your spiritual side as well. Having a connection with and do something that's greater than yourself can provide you with a sense of purpose and make you feel stronger from within. Get in touch with your spirituality, and you will be able to find some peace. It doesn't mean that you have to spend hours together meditating or anything of that sort. Just take some time out and go to a place of worship, meditate for 15 minutes, or go for a walk and admire the nature. Do anything that makes you feel closer to the cosmos.

Method Three:
Developing Mental and Emotional Strength

Start setting reasonable goals

You can start developing your mental strength by setting reasonable goals for yourself. It is not just about setting goals, but it is about taking the necessary steps to achieving your goals as well. If you want to start working towards your goals, you will need to start applying yourself. It means that you will have to ask yourself even when you are bored or going through some turmoil, and sticking to the plan until you have accomplished the goals you have set for yourself. It will not be an easy feat and don't let it scare you. Practice makes a man perfect, and this age-old adage is true! Keep practicing, and you will get better! If you have set some big goals for yourself and they seem impossible, try breaking them down into manageable steps that are doable. For instance, if you want to become assertive, then your first step should be to learn to speak up for yourself at least thrice every week. These instances could be major or minor one. But you will have to speak up for yourself. Develop a "stick with it" mindset. Even if you face an obstacle or a setback, keep trying and don't give up. Start being resilient and don't worry about the troubles you come across. The goal is to keep going till you have achieved what you wanted to. Think of all the failures as an opportunity to learn and please do learn from them. Every day is a new day and don't let the troubles from your past sneak up on you.

Don't let negativity get a hold on you

Negativity can sneak up on you quite quickly. It can be stemmed from a negative emotion that you are harboring within yourself or it could be because of something external like negative feedback or toxic people around you. While certain things are beyond your control, the one thing that you can control is the way you feel about yourself and your life. Don't let any negativity live within you. You cannot control what others think about you, but you can certainly control the way you feel about yourself. There are different ways in which you can manage all the negativity. You can start by identifying and challenging such negative thoughts. You can reduce your interaction with harmful and toxic people. If you think you are in a toxic relationship, learn to break free of it. Don't entertain negativity in any form. If a person doesn't contribute to your growth or well being and instead brings you down, stay away from such a person at all costs. At times, you will have to interact with people who are negative, and you cannot avoid such meetings. In such a situation, set some boundaries and don't let their words get to you. Don't take everything personally.

Positive self-talk

Make use of positive self-talk to build up your mental strength. Making use of positive affirmations will help you in developing a positive outlook while getting rid of all negativity around you. Take a couple of minutes and look at yourself in the mirror and say something positive and motivating to yourself. You can say something that you believe in or something that you would like to be true to yourself. A couple of positive affirmations that you can make use of are: "I am working on becoming emotionally stronger", "I am learning to manage my stress effectively, and I'll be kind to myself", "I am working on achieving my goals, and I will continue to do so", or anything else that you can think of.

Stay calm even under pressure

Whenever you feel that a particular situation is escalating quickly, and you feel that your emotions are going to boil over, learn to keep your cool. When you learn to control your emotions instead of letting them control you, you are giving yourself an opportunity to weigh in your options before deciding on a particular choice. Take a minute, count to ten, before you let a negative emotion boil over. This might sound like a cliché, but it does work. Before having an emotional reaction towards something, take a moment to gather your thoughts and react accordingly. You can try practicing meditation as well, and it can help you in maintaining your calm. Meditation can help you in staying objective while providing you with the necessary time to make sense of your thoughts and emotions. Instead of reacting immediately, you can weigh in your thoughts and emotions and then think of your next step.

Letting go of petty things

If you are always sensitive to the petty annoyances and verbal barbs or taunts that we all tend to come across daily, then you will end up becoming quite bitter. Also, you will be wasting a lot of your precious time and energy thinking about unnecessary things, which don't matter at the end of the day. When you start spending time thinking about all such things and start paying attention to them, you are making them a significant problem that will increase your stress. Learning to adjust your attitude can help you in letting these petty and trivial issues go without increasing your level of stress. You are not only preventing the wastage of your valuable time and energy, but you are also saving yourself the trouble of having to deal with extra stress. Instead of stressing yourself out about all these things, you should develop a healthy routine of thinking about the things that are bothering you, then take a deep breath, calm yourself down, and once you are calm, think of the best way in which you can deal with that issue. For instance, if your spouse keeps forgetting to put the cap on the tube of toothpaste after using it, you should understand that such a thing isn't as important to your partner as it is to you. If this bothers you, think about all the other things that your partner does for you that make you feel good and in comparison, you can certainly let this small flaw of hers go. Don't try to be a perfectionist, at least not all the time. When you do this, you are setting high expectations for yourself, and these tend to be entirely unrealistic. Try to be realistic while thinking about things and don't let the idea of perfection create any additional stress or burden. You can make use of a straightforward visualization exercise that will help you in letting go of little things that seem to be bothering you. Take a small stone or pebble and hold it in your hand. Transfer all your negative thoughts that are bothering you into that pebble. And once you are ready, swing it as hard as you can or toss it into a pond. Visualize that all the petty problems are drowning along with the pebble that's sinking. You are casting away all your negative emotions.

Changing your perspective

We tend to get so caught up in our problems that we tend to look at things from a different perspective. A fresh perspective towards existing troubles can help in solving your problems. If you feel like you have hit a dead end with something, take a break and relax. Once you feel refreshed, start thinking of ways in which you can tackle that problem. If you change the way in which you are approaching a problem, you might find a solution to it in no time. Here are couple of different things that you can try to get a new perspective on things.

Start reading. Reading the daily news or a book can help you in stepping into someone else's world, and this serves as a good reminder to let you know that the world is a vast place and that your problems are nothing significant when you think about the entirety of the universe we live in. You can start volunteering. When you start interacting with others who could use your help, you certainly will get a different perspective of how things are. Ask your friend for some advice if you feel lost and make sure that you are thinking about the advice your friend gives you. Step out of your comfort zone and start traveling. It will certainly help you in getting things in perspective.

Maintaining a positive outlook

All those who are mentally as well as emotionally strong tend to be happy with what they have. They usually have a positive outlook towards life and don't complain much.

This doesn't mean that they don't have any problems. Of course, they have problems just like everyone else, but the difference between them and everyone else is that they can see the bigger picture and know that the challenges they are facing are a part of life. Maintaining a positive outlook towards life will provide you with the mental and the emotional strength that you will need to tackle any problem you come across. Remember that bad times will pass, and the good times are just around the corner. Don't lose hope in the meanwhile.

Being honest with yourself

The ability to face reality is a sign of your mental and emotional strength. If you are going to overcome a hurdle or a challenge, then you should be able to tackle it head-on. Lying to yourself about your troubles won't make them go away, and you will just end up hurting yourself in the process. If you overeat when you are stressed or sad, accept the fact that there is a problem that needs to be addressed. Don't look for a means of escape and try being honest with yourself.

Method Four: Dealing with Life

Start thinking before acting

Whenever you feel that you are stuck in a difficult situation, take a while to think things through. Don't react instantly and don't be in a hurry to make a decision. It will provide you with sufficient time for your emotions to diffuse and you can start weighing in your options with an open mind. It is important that you do this, regardless of the situation you are in. If you can afford to, then take some time and list down the pros and cons of a situation. Make a note of how you are feeling as well. Try finding some positive points about the situation you are in, and this can help in changing your perspective towards things. At times, the smallest change in perception can make a huge difference. Follow the ten-second rule. Give yourself ten seconds for something to sink in before expressing yourself. Even if your partner tells you that he or she wants to end the relationship, take ten seconds to compose yourself and then respond.

Examining all the alternatives

Once you have managed to compose yourself, before you decide on the course of action, think clearly about the circumstance you are in. What happened and what are the possible options available to you? There will always be more than one path that you can opt for. For instance, let us assume that your friend asked you to do something morally wrong and you are torn between your loyalty to your friend and your sense of morality. So, now you will need to weigh in the different pros and cons and decide accordingly.

Select the right path and stick to it

Make use of your inner voice or your conscience to guide you. Trust your instincts, and you are likely to be correct. At times, the answer might be quite clear and distinct, but it might be hard to do the right thing. Do not let the problem fester into a more significant hassle than the one it already is. You need to take a call and stick to it. You can always ask others for an opinion and weigh their opinions before concluding. However, remember that it needs to be your own decision and no one else's. Since you are the one who will have to live with the consequences of it. If you feel like you are stuck, think about what someone you admire would do in such a situation. The decision that you take should be something that you can live with. And don't do something because someone thinks that it is a good idea. Do it because you want to.

Reflect on your experiences

Once a problematic situation passes you by, think about the way in which you dealt with it and the outcome of that situation. Would you like to change something about the way you dealt with it or are you proud of yourself? Remember that wisdom is derived from practice. Examining what happened and the way you dealt with it will help you in making any changes the next time you have to deal with a similar situation. If things worked out for you, then it is all good. However, if things didn't exactly go as you planned, even that's all right. You had a chance to learn, and that's what it was. It was a learning experience, and you will be careful in future.

CHAPTER 9:
ESSENTIAL TRAITS

In this chapter, you will learn about the different traits that you should work on developing if you want to be mentally tough. There are various tips that you could make use of to develop the concerned trait.

Self-confidence

In this section, you will learn about the different tips that you can make use of for developing your self-confidence.

Invest your energy carefully

Ask yourself an elementary question, "What is the worst that could happen." More often than not, we tend to place a lot of importance on "likely" or potential problems. Our energy reserves are finite, so instead of wasting it all on worrying about hypothetical problems, why don't you concentrate on building and developing your personal and professional relationships? Spend your energy on positive and important things like your personal and professional goals that you would like to achieve. If you are really worried about something, then why don't you take some action to correct the problem or minimizing the risk? Be careful while investing your energy and time.

Visualization can help

If you are doing something for the first time, then visualize that you have done that task in the past. Close your eyes for a moment and conjure up a vivid image where you have succeeded in doing what you are doing now for the first time. The mind doesn't know the difference between a vivid imagination and something that's real. So, make your imagination as vivid as you possibly can.

Try copying others

Find a role model for yourself and observe their attitude and behavior. Try adapting all their positive qualities while letting go of the negative ones. Try being as confident as that person seems to be. How can you do this? Try talking to them, provided you have access. If you cannot talk to them, try gathering as much information as you can about them.

"As-if"

Try making use of the "as-if" frame of mind. This is quite simple. Imagine that you are a self-confident individual and think about the manner in which you would approach a given situation. How would you behave? How would you move? How would you talk? And what would you be thinking? When you do this, you are encouraging yourself to put yourself in a state of mind where you are self-assured and quite confident. Do this often, and within no time, you will start feeling confident as well.

Step into the future

Take a peek into the future and ask your "future" self if the problem that you have to overcome is as difficult as you think it is. At times, the problem might not be difficult or even complicated. We tend to complicate it. Make use of the 5*5 rule. Take a moment and think about whether the problem that you are faced with would matter to you five years down the line. If your answer is no, then it isn't worth wasting 5 minutes of your time. At times a slight change in perspective can be really helpful.

Let go of the negative internal self-talk

Self-talk is useful only when it is positive. Negative self-talk can make you feel quite low. Ignore the nagging internal voice that isn't positive. You have the option of listening to it or ignoring it. So, decide carefully. If the voice is bothering you, mute it! After all, it is in your head. So, you can decide whether you want to listen to it or not.

Self-confidence is a beautiful accessory, and when you are confident in yourself, you will be able to think more clearly and decide rationally. Self-confidence also helps in improving your mental toughness.

Self-motivation

You can start out in a straightforward manner. You can motivate yourself by placing motivators around your workstation. Motivators are the things that keep you going; elements that provide the initial spark. Things like a family photograph, an inspirational quote, a picture of an exotic destination you want to visit and so on. Always keep good company. Your circle can have a positive or a negative impact on the way you think and behave. Surround yourself with happy and optimistic people, and you will feel optimistic. Never stop learning and keep reading. When you start learning more, you are bound to feel more confident about yourself. Don't let negativity get to you. Maintain a positive outlook towards life in general. Look for the good in bad! If you find that you don't have the necessary motivation to do something, then you should perhaps set that project aside for a while and get started on something else. This will help you in building some momentum. Once you have gained some momentum, you can go back to the previous project. The more you keep telling yourself that you aren't supposed to think about something, the more time you will spend thinking about it.

It is how the human psyche tends to work. It becomes almost impossible to not think about it! The trick is not to let this happen. When you feel yourself leaning towards postponing something for a while, you should try and avoid it. Just shift your attention towards something else. For instance, instead of thinking that you aren't supposed to procrastinate, try thinking about how good you will feel once you have completed the task. In this manner, you will be able to take the necessary action instead of worrying about a specific behavior.

Keep track of times when you feel motivated and the times when you feel like giving up. There will be a specific pattern in it, and once you know the pattern, you can find a way to work around it. Keep track of your progress. You can make a progress bar, and when you see it grow, you will want to keep nurturing it, and it will keep you motivated. When you are motivated, it is easier to accomplish things. It is even easier when the motivation comes from within and is not dependent on someone else. You can help others as well!

Stop procrastinating

The act of intentionally putting something off for a later date even though it should be done right away is known as procrastination. Not all procrastination is negative. For instance, if you rush off to your yoga class before starting a new project at work will make you feel energetic for the new challenge. Maybe you like cleaning and organizing your room before you start studying. These habits are not harmful and will help in preparing yourself for the challenge that lies ahead. However, if procrastination is wreaking havoc on your personal and professional life, then it obviously isn't constructive. Once you have decided whether it is constructive or destructive, you will need to identify the underlying cause for procrastination. Here are the most common reasons.

- Drama: It can be quite exciting to procrastinate, waiting until the very last minute to complete a task can feel like you are gambling against all odds. You are betting on yourself that you will be able to pull it off and the things that aren't in your control (reaction of your coworkers, the copy machine, or even the highway traffic), will work in your favor. So, procrastination can create drama in your life that might make things seem interesting, and this might feel better than going about doing things promptly.
- The fear of failure: If you wait until the very last to perform a task, then you can always claim that you could have done better had there been more time. Procrastination helps in providing yourself with an excuse when things don't work in your favor.
- Fear of success as well: Being afraid of success is quite real. Maybe you are worried that your responsibilities will increase if you perform well. This fear might deter you from performing well. In fact, you are effectively sabotaging yourself and your career.
- Perfectionism: You are your worst enemy. Trying to be a perfectionist will prevent you from completing

a task. It is almost impossible to live up to the standards that you have created for yourself, and this will demotivate you from even starting.

- Hostile feelings towards someone: Perhaps you resent the person that assigned you the work, and by procrastinating you are merely channelizing your hostility towards them. When you don't like whom you work for, it is very likely that you wouldn't want to do the things assigned to them.
- Lack of interest: Perhaps the task that you are put up to is boring, or it doesn't interest you. Or maybe you don't have any personal interest vested in its outcome or result.
- Task seems confusing: Maybe you don't understand something about the task on hand. Or maybe it looks unmanageable and you don't know where to start from or even organize it.

It is important to determine the reason for procrastination. Once you know the reason, you can try to rectify it.

Focus

Your level of mental toughness depends on your ability to stay focused. If you can stay focused, only then will you be able to achieve your goals? In this section, you will learn about the different tips that you can follow to stay focused.

Getting some exercise is important

Physical activity is essential to improve your ability to focus and concentrate. Exercising or any other form of physical activity helps in releasing chemicals that enable the brain to learn and remember. Exercising is so much better than a cup of coffee. It can provide you with a boost of energy that improves your mental and cognitive functioning. Thereby making it easy for you to stay focused.

Staying hydrated

Did you know that mild dehydration could lead to wavering of your attention? Yes, it does! So, make it a point to have at least 8 cups of water per day. Keep drinking plenty of fluids. If your consumption of coffee is high, then increase your water intake accordingly.

The important things in life

Take a couple of minutes and think about all the things that are important to you in your life. What are the tasks or chores that cause you a lot of worry and stress? Now, think about whether you think these tasks are important to you. If the things that stress you out the most aren't amongst the list of important things, you can safely stop stressing over them. By getting rid of such unnecessary tensions, you can start focusing on things that are important to you. Once you know where you need to focus, you can start breaking down those important things into smaller functions that are manageable.

Getting rid of all distractions

Technology is the cornerstone of the world that we live in these days. Technology has provided us with the ability to stay connected with everyone, regardless of where you are. Technology has plenty of advantages. However, one of the major disadvantages is that it is a distraction. So, technology does lead to inattention, and it diffuses your focus as well. It is highly unlikely that you will be able to concentrate on something if your phone keeps buzzing constantly! So, get rid of all your gadgets and gizmos when you are trying to concentrate on something. It is a common habit to wake up in the morning and immediately check your texts, emails and social media updates. Your mind tends to be fresh, and your ability to concentrate is quite high in the morning. When you squander away this energy on trivial things, you are hurting your productivity.

Working on one thing at a time

Don't try to multitask. If you want to accomplish something, then focus on that one thing alone. If you try to multitask, you are spreading your attention on multiple things, and you will not be able to give it your best shot. Learn to prioritize your tasks and start with the ones that are your top priority and work your way down the list.

Taking small steps

If your goal is to lose weight, then you will need to start taking small steps that will help you in achieving your goal. You cannot achieve a goal if you don't focus on the little things that are equally important. If you want to lose weight, you shouldn't just concentrate on getting physical exercise. You need to make sure that you are eating healthy food, you are getting sufficient sleep, and you are exercising too.

Prioritizing

Making a to-do list is very helpful. Take a paper and make a note of all the things that you have to do on a particular day. You have two options when it comes to making a to-do list. You can either make this list early in the morning or before going to bed on the previous night. When you have a to-do list prepared, you don't have to worry about running around like a headless chicken and will have a sense of direction. When you have a sense of course, you can start working towards achieving the goals you have set for yourself. When you know what you have to achieve, you can set aside all the other distractions and instead focus on your goals. When you see the tasks that you need to complete, there is no room for distractions. You can develop your mental strength if you have goals.

CHAPTER 10:
CRITICAL THINKING

Making use of "wasted" time

We all tend to waste time; that is, we all fail to properly utilize all the time that we have at our disposal. At times we simply flit from one kind of diversion to the next one, without actually enjoying any of those activities. At times, we tend to get irritated about matters that are well beyond our control and are known as external factors. At times, we don't have a proper plan of action and this, in turn, causes a domino effect with plenty of negative consequences that could have very well been avoided. How many times did you get stuck in horrible rush hour traffic that you could have probably avoided had you just left an hour earlier! Apart from all the time that we while away without doing anything, we start worrying about all sorts of unnecessary things. Sometimes we regret the way we behaved or acted in the past, or we just end up daydreaming about all the things that you wish you had done differently if you could;

instead, of putting in some effort to achieve the desired results. Well, you need to understand that you will not get all that time back and it is all in the past. Instead, you should try focusing on all the time that you have right now. One way in which you can develop your ability to think critically is by making use of all the time that would have otherwise have been "wasted." Instead of spending an hour flipping through channels on TV without enjoying it, you can perhaps make use of this time for self-introspection. You can also try and reflect about the day you had, the things you did, and all that you have to do still. Spend this time to contemplate about your productivity. Here are a couple of questions that you can ask yourself:

What was the highlight of my day? When was I most and least efficient today? What did I keep thinking about all day long? Do I have a solution to the problem I was thinking about? Have I reached a logical conclusion? Did I spend any time thinking negative thoughts? If I had the chance of repeating this day all over again, is there anything about it that I would like to change? Did I do something that will help me in achieving my goals?

Take some time out of your busy schedule and answer these questions and record your observations.

One problem per day

Make it a daily habit of yours to select one issue that you would like to work on during the day. Identify the different components of the said problem and think of a logical solution to it. To state it simply, you will need to go through these questions systematically: What is the actual problem? How does this issue obstruct my goals? Once you have thought about these questions, here are the steps that you can follow to solve the problem.

When possible, try to tackle one problem after the other, in order. Go in an order and don't try to solve more than one issue at any given point of time. State the problem as clearly as you can and then study the problem. For instance, you will need to figure out the kind of the issues that you can and cannot solve. There will be certain things that you have control over and others that you cannot control. Concentrate on the problems that you can solve and the ones that are within your control. Let go of everything else and don't waste your time and energy over such issues. Think about the information you will need and start searching for it. After gathering the necessary information, analyze and interpret it for coming to a logical conclusion. Think of the various short and long-term solutions for the said problem. Once you are aware of all the available options, you will need to weigh each of these options. Evaluate their pros and cons. After doing this, select a path and follow it.

Internalizing intellectual standards

Certain intellectual standards are accepted universally, and they consist of clarity, precision, accuracy, relevance, depth, breadth, logic, and significance. Every week, you should select any one of these standards and try to increase your awareness of it. For instance, you can select clarity and work on it for a week, then shift towards precision, and so on. If you are focusing on transparency, notice the manner in which you communicate with others and see if you are clear or not. Also, observe when others are and aren't being clear while communicating. Whenever you are reading, see if you have clarity about what you are learning. While you are expressing yourself orally or through writing, check to see if you are being clear in expressing yourself. There are four simple things that you can use to check whether you are clear or not. State explicitly what you are trying to say, elaborate and then make use of examples for better understanding, and use some analogies. So, you are supposed to state, elaborate, illustrate, and exemplify what you are trying to say to ensure clarity in communication.

Maintain a journal

Start maintaining an intellectual journal wherein you record certain observations every week. The first step is to write about any situation that you care about or that you think was significant. After doing this, record the way you responded to that situation. Try being as accurate as you possibly can be. Once this is done, then move on to analyzing that case. The final step is to assess that situation and think about all the things that you would do differently if you get a do-over.

Reshaping your character

Select an intellectual trait such as perseverance, empathy, independence, courage, or anything else of this sort. Once you have carefully chosen a trait, try to focus on it for a month and try to develop it. If the quality you have selected is humility, then start noticing those situations where you admit that you are wrong and where you don't. Notice if you refuse to accept your mistake, even if the evidence states that you were wrong. Notice when you become defensive when someone tries to correct your behavior or tell you when you are wrong. Observe when your arrogance is getting the better of you and is preventing you from learning something new. Whenever you notice yourself indulging in any form of negative behavior or negative thinking, squash all those thoughts. Start reshaping your character and start inculcating desirable behavioral traits and give up on the negative ones. Learn to let go of everything that's negative.

Dealing with your egocentrism

We are all inherently egocentric. While pondering something, we tend to subliminally support ourselves and give ourselves precedence over others. Indeed, we are biased towards ourselves. You can see your egocentric behavior at least once a day by considering the questions mentioned below.

Name the circumstances under which you would invariably favor yourself? Do you become irritable over little things? Did you do or say something that is obviously "irrational" for the sake of getting your way? Did you try to impose your opinion on others? Did you fail to speak your mind out about something that you feel strongly for and then regret not doing it later on? Once you have identified these egocentric traits, you can start actively working on rationalizing them. Whenever you feel like you are egocentric, think about the way in which a rational person would react in a similar situation and see how that compares to the way in which you are behaving.

Redefining the way in which you see things

The world that we live in is social and private; all the situations we come across are already "defined." The manner in which a situation is defined not only determines your feelings towards it, but the way you act, and its consequences. However, every circumstance can be defined in numerous ways. It means that you are in fact holding the key to your happiness. It implies that all those situations to which you have attached a negative meaning can be easily transformed into something positive if you want to do so. This strategy is about finding something positive in everything that seems to be negative to you. It is all about your perception of how things are. If you think that something is positive, then it will be so and vice versa.

Get in touch with your emotions

Whenever you start feeling some negative emotion, ask yourself the following:

What are the thoughts that have led to this particular emotion? For instance, if you are angry, then ask yourself, what were you thinking about that made you angry? What are the other ways in which you can view that particular situation? Every situation is different depending on your perspective. If you have a negative outlook towards life, everything will seem bleak and dull. A positive outlook, on the other hand, can brighten things up considerably.

Analyzing the influence of a group on your life

Carefully observe the way your behavior is influenced by the team that you are a part of. Your behavior is bound to change depending on whom you are around. Well, if you want to become mentally tough, then you shouldn't let your behavior change because of someone else.

CHAPTER 11:
SETTING GOALS

Well, how do you decide about the things that you should and shouldn't focus on? Well, this is where goals come into the picture. Goals are your objectives, and they help in defining the things that you would like to achieve in your life. You can have short term, medium term, and long-term goals. Depending on the things you want to achieve and how you want to achieve them, your goals will change.

Always start with the ideal situation

Now, this is your chance to dream. Imagine that you have a blank paper in front of you and you have the power as well as the opportunity to decide who you would want to be and what you would want to do. Don't start worrying about all the obstacles you might face along the way; all that comes later on. You simply have to dream right now, let your imagination run wild. There might be numerous things that you want to do. Start with the possibilities and then you can check to see if it is viable. Don't worry about all the bills, the mortgages, or other burdens while you are dreaming. Think about the ideal version of "you," and then you will have to think of the possible ways in which you can turn your dreams into reality.

Always write down your goals

When you start making a note of all your goals, you will begin seeing the direction you would like to head in, and this makes the process of decision making simple. It might sound pretty old school or conventional, but writing down your goals is quite useful. People usually like keeping everything in their brain instead of writing it all down. When you write something down, it helps in lending that goal a sense of clarity. Once you have written down all your goals down you should place that paper in a place where you can see it daily. It will serve as a reminder of the things that you ought to achieve, and you will subconsciously start thinking about your goals. It will provide you with a sense of purpose.

Determine its importance

You need to be quite clear when it comes to setting goals for yourself. Why is that particular goal important for you? Why is it significant? Is it important because your spouse/partner/or family members want you to do it or because you want to? Your goals shouldn't fall under the "should be" category. Well, there are various things that you "should be" doing according to others and the society. Instead, think about the things that you want to do; the things you are doing for yourself. For instance, your goal is to shed a few kilos. Now, why is this important for you? Will you take the necessary steps and make the necessary sacrifices to attain this goal you have set? Making difficult choices is a part of the process of setting goals. So, you will need to start prioritizing.

The basic question that you need to answer is whether you will feel a sense of achievement when you have in fact achieved that goal. For instance, you might have set a goal of becoming the best business in your niche market. But if you want to stay connected to your child and coach your child's football team, achieving your business goal might or might not leave you feeling satisfied and happy. Yes, you do have to consider such questions regardless of how tough or unfair they seem. So, sit down and start thinking seriously. Don't worry about what you are writing; just write everything down. Here are a couple of questions that you can ask yourself to figure out the important things in your life.

What would you do if you only had six months left to live? What would you do if you never had to worry about your finances and could do whatever you wanted? What would you do if you knew that you would never fail, regardless of what you want to do?

Once you have answered these questions, forget about it for the next 24 hours. Come back later on and see how you feel about the things that you have written down. Whatever still makes sense to you should be left as it is and the rest can be discarded.

Your goals should add some meaning to your life

The goals that you have set for yourself should never be vague. A vague goal can make you lose track of the things you have to accomplish, faster than anything else. If you want to become a better swimmer, start exercising regularly, or become a better leader, then your goal needs to be specific in that regard. Say your goal out loud and be honest with yourself about whether it gives you any clarity about what it is and isn't. Once you have a clear goal, then you have to make sure that it is something that you care about. Many goals might seem specific but are very vague. For instance, a target that says getting in shape doesn't specify whether you are trying to lose weight, improve your stamina, or reduce your cholesterol levels. Getting in shape is very vague. Instead, a goal that says, "I want to lose 20 pounds in 4 months" is a specific goal. Building a business is an example of a vague goal along with spending quality time with friends. The more uncertain your goal happens, the more likely it is that you will abandon it. A specific goal will provide you with a sense of purpose.

Prioritize and pursue your goal

It is very likely that you will have several important things in your life that you want to do. So, make a list of all your goals and then select the three most important goals. These three goals are referred to as your tier-one goals: the ones that have the potential of altering your life. They aren't necessarily the goals that will help you in churning money easily or earn you fame, but they are the goals that will provide your life with some meaning. These goals can be big or small and could be something like changing your profession, completing your education, or paying off your student debts. The only condition is that the goals mentioned in tier-one should be of some significance to you.

Create a reward system

Always create a reward system for yourself. Regardless of whether you have completed a small or a big task, you should always reward yourself to complete your work. The reward system doesn't have to be an elaborate one. For instance, you can treat yourself to a cup of coffee once you have reviewed your emails in the morning. This small reward will provide you with the necessary motivation to complete the task. Always enjoy your victories, big or small it doesn't matter. A sense of accomplishment will help you to keep going. This will help in developing a positive attitude towards your work and will provide you with the necessary motivation to keep going. Striking off simple things from your to-do list can be quite satisfactory. If you like making to-do lists, then you will undoubtedly understand the happiness of striking elements off from that list.

Less is more

The more goals that you have, the less time and energy you will be able to dedicate towards each of those goals. So, learn to limit the number of goals that you have set for yourself. Resist the temptation of setting multiple goals. If you are interested, you can set numerous goals, provided that you are willing to work on only one goal at a time. Don't try to multitask when it comes to achieving your goals. One single goal would be great because it means that you will be able to dedicate all your time, energy, and focus towards that goal without any distractions.

Option to go public or staying private

When you tell someone about your goals, you are unknowingly increasing your accountability. It is likely that you will finish a task if you have already told someone about it. You get to decide whom you want to discuss it with. Accountability towards someone else will make you want to complete the task on hand. It is entirely up to you whether you want to go public or stay private about your goals. If you like the idea of having others to provide you support and motivation to keep going, then share about your goals with those who matter to you.

Plan of action

A goal without a plan of action is worthless. It is good that you know what you want. However, what good is an objective if you don't do anything to achieve it? A goal is worthless on its own. You can add value to it only if you take steps to achieving it. You certainly don't have to know all the steps well in advance. You need to have a fair idea of the direction you are headed in and should be aware of the steps that you can take for achieving those goals. Spend some time and create a plan of action for yourself. Learn to plan your day efficiently so that you are making the most of the time that you have at your disposal.

Adjust and adapt

You can certainly have a specific goal for yourself, and you probably have also devised a strategy that will assist you in achieving those goals. Well, your approach should allow for changes and adjustments. At times you will need to re-evaluate your plans, re-trace your steps, and overcome certain obstacles that you couldn't or didn't foresee. All these things will take up extra time and might delay the attainment of your goals. So, leave some space in your plans for adjustments. Your ideas shouldn't be rigid, and they should be flexible. After all, we live in a dynamic world where things keep changing! So, your plan to achieve your goals might need to be tweaked at times.

It is important to have goals for yourself if you want to become successful in your life. Goals will not only give you a sense of purpose but will help you in strengthening yourself mentally as well. When you know what your purpose is, all that you need to do is go about achieving it. You aren't giving yourself any time to waste on unnecessary activities and thoughts. You can streamline your day and your thinking process as well. Instead of contemplating about trivial things, you can focus your mental abilities towards achieving the goals you have defined for yourself. The thought of having to make a to-do list daily does sound cumbersome. Find a method that works well for you. The aim is to set goals. The method that you employ to accomplish this task doesn't matter. Make it a habit of setting goals for yourself. Doing this regularly will help in improving your level of confidence as well and provide you with some sense of control over your life. It helps in getting things in motion when you have predefined goals. Make sure that the goals you have set for yourself are specific and not vague.

Conclusion

I would like to thank you for purchasing this book.

By now you would have realized the importance of being mentally tough. If you want to be successful in life and attain peace, then you should learn to let go. Learn to let go of all the things that you cannot control, the things that others say and do. Your happiness lies in your hands and no one can take it away from you. If you let other's actions, words, and opinions bother you, then you need to change that about yourself as soon as possible. You aren't someone else's puppet but are the master of your own destiny and happiness. Don't let anyone tell you any different.

In this book, you learnt about the different tips that you can follow to develop a tough mental attitude. The tips are quite simple to follow, but you need to put in considerable effort! Don't forget that patience is the corner stone to develop mental toughness. This isn't a process that can take place overnight. It will take conscious effort, hard work, and time! Moreover, you certainly shouldn't feel disheartened if you don't see any immediate results. It is a lifelong process and it keeps going on. So, what are you waiting for? Take the first step today and start working on yourself!

Thank you and all the best!

Made in the USA
Middletown, DE
25 March 2018